To Judy & Roger — the happy couple — Congratulations!

from

Hugo, Carol, Lucy, and Amanda

with love

TIME'S RIVER

The Voyage of Life in Art and Poetry

poetry and art selected by Kate Farrell

National Gallery of Art, Washington
A Bulfinch Press Book / Little, Brown and Company
Boston • New York • London

First edition

See page 119 for artists' copyrights and credits.

All translations are by Kate Farrell except as noted.

ISBN 0-8212-2507-3

Library of Congress Catalogue Card Number 98-74805

Endpapers: From Peter Flötner, *Moresques and Damasquines,* 1546,
bound volume with engravings
Pages 10, 36, 64, 92: Thomas Cole, *The Voyage of Life* (details), 1842

Acknowledgments
I am particularly grateful to Carol Eron, editor at the National Gallery
of Art. Carol's steadfast commitment made the book possible; her
superb orchestration of its many elements made it a reality. Thanks
also to Mariah Shay for her able editorial assistance. And a special
thanks to Donald Sanders, whose play *Thomas Cole: A Waking Dream*
first inspired my enthusiasm for Cole's *Voyage of Life* series.   KF

Bulfinch Press is an imprint and trademark of Little, Brown and
Company (Inc.).

PRINTED IN SINGAPORE

Down Time's quaint stream
Without an oar
We are enforced to sail
Our Port a secret
Our Perchance a Gale
What Skipper would
Incur the Risk
What Buccaneer would ride
Without a surety from the Wind
Or schedule of the Tide—

> *Emily Dickinson*

THIS BOOK IS DEDICATED TO MY PARENTS
RAYMOND AND EILEEN DOUGHERTY

Contents

Wishing for the Cloths of Heaven

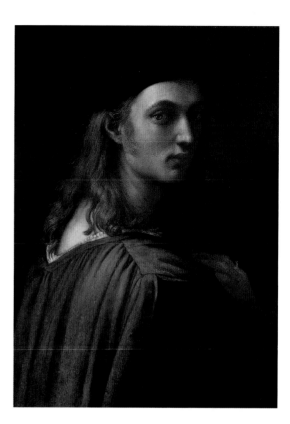

Midway through the Journey

In Age I Bud Again

Introduction

THE INSPIRATION for this book is *The Voyage of Life*, Thomas
Cole's four-part allegorical series of paintings hanging in the
National Gallery of Art. In Cole's famous sequence, a traveler
sails down a wondrous river through supernatural landscapes
that represent the four stages of life. Organized around Cole's
paintings, this anthology unites masterpieces from the National
Gallery of Art with poems from around the world about life's
journey—its changing hopes and pleasures; loves and losses;
struggles, turning points, and inner victories. In keeping with
Cole's idea, the works are arranged so that turning the book's pages unfolds the story, at
once individual and universal, of growing up and older.

In the four sections introduced by Cole's paintings are poems about childhood
(*How Like an Angel Came I Down!*), young adulthood (*Wishing for the Cloths of
Heaven*), maturity (*Midway through the Journey*), and old age (*In Age I Bud Again*).
The poems come from diverse times and places and express all sorts of outlooks,
circumstances, and inspirations. Some explicitly describe a particular time of life,
as do Anne Porter's magical memory of infancy and Dante's classic lines about midlife
despair. Those less specific about age appear in the sections where they seem to fit best.
Emily Dickinson's "Hope Is the Thing with Feathers" is in the second section;
Jane Kenyon's "Otherwise" in the last—though Kenyon died before reaching old age.
Echoing a premise of Cole's *Voyage of Life* paintings, many poems link outer loss and
physical aging with inner renewal and transformation, a theme summed up
by saying that the spirit grows younger as the body grows older.

Combining the poetry with art that conveys so many kinds of moods and moments allows a flow of scenes and viewpoints that suggests both the evanescence of our voyage and the inner distances we travel as we get older. Thus, the life-long odyssey of love that threads through the book—in poems by Rabindranath Tagore, Robert Hayden, Li Po, Robert Bly, Saint Paul, and Walt Whitman, among others—leads, in turn, through domestic settings by Marc Chagall and Horace Pippin, across Fitz Hugh Lane's luminous seas, into a quiet French garden by Edouard Vuillard, through an imaginary landscape by Sassetta, culminating in Claude Monet's magnificent river sunset. Meanwhile, powerful mythic and religious images reflect the spiritual vicissitudes of the journey—visions by Edvard Munch, William Blake, Georges de la Tour, and Henri Matisse, for instance, illustrate poetic epiphanies by Anna Swir; Makeda, Queen of Sheba; Goethe; and Hyongson Kim, respectively.

In one of the book's final poems, Jorge Luis Borges compares art to an endless river, one that mirrors the flow of our ever-changing lives. This collection is meant to evoke both rivers, with the hope that a journey through its pages may help illuminate the mystery whereby individual uniqueness combines with common human stages to make an ordinary life seem a miracle of pattern and destiny.

KATE FARRELL

How Like an Angel Came I Down!

William Blake, from *Songs of Innocence*, 1789

Infant Joy

I have no name:
I am but two days old.
What shall I call thee?
I happy am,
Joy is my name.
Sweet joy befall thee!

Pretty joy!
Sweet joy but two days old,
Sweet joy I call thee:
Thou dost smile,
I sing the while,
Sweet joy befall thee!

William Blake, English, 1757–1827

Our Birth Is But a Sleep and a Forgetting

FROM *Ode: Intimations of Immortality*
From Recollections of Early Childhood

Our birth is but a sleep and a forgetting:
The Soul that rises with us, our life's Star,
    Hath had elsewhere its setting,
        And cometh from afar:
    Not in entire forgetfulness,
    And not in utter nakedness,
But trailing clouds of glory do we come
        From God, who is our home:
Heaven lies about us in our infancy!
Shades of the prison-house begin to close
    Upon the growing Boy,
But He beholds the light, and whence it flows,
    He sees it in his joy;
The Youth, who daily farther from the east
    Must travel, still is Nature's Priest,
    And by the vision splendid
    Is on his way attended;
At length the Man perceives it die away,
And fade into the light of common day.

William Wordsworth, English, 1770–1850

Claude Monet, *The Cradle—Camille with
the Artist's Son Jean,* 1867

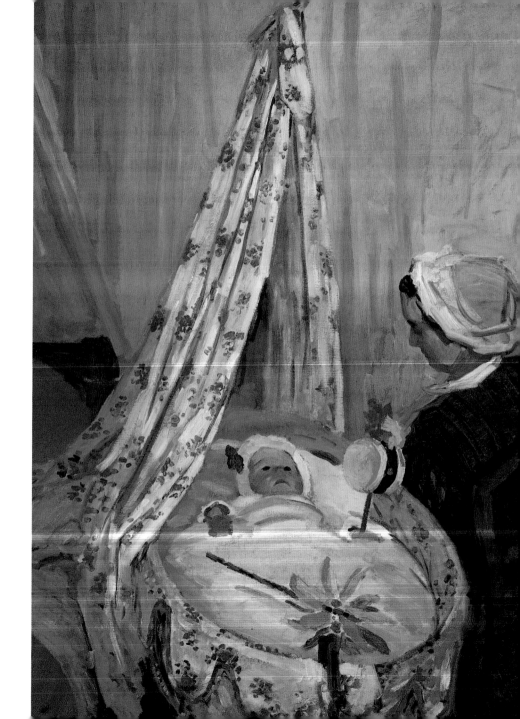

Marc Chagall, *Féla and Odilon*, 1915

The Beginning

"Where have I come from, where did you
pick me up?" the baby asked its mother.

She answered, half crying, half laughing,
and clasping the baby to her breast,—

"You were hidden in my heart as its desire,
my darling.

You were in the dolls of my childhood's
games; and when with clay I made the image
of my god every morning, I made and unmade
you then.

You were enshrined with our household
deity, in his worship I worshipped you.

In all my hopes and my loves, in my life,
in the life of my mother you have lived.

In the lap of the deathless Spirit who rules
our home you have been nursed for ages.

When in girlhood my heart was opening
its petals, you hovered as a fragrance about it.

Your tender softness bloomed in my
youthful limbs, like a glow in the sky before sunrise.

Heaven's first darling, twin-born with
the morning's light, you have floated down
the stream of the world's life, and at last you
have stranded on my heart.

As I gaze on your face, mystery overwhelms
me; you who belong to all have become mine.

For fear of losing you I hold you tight to my
breast. What magic has snared the world's
treasure in these slender arms of mine?"

Rabindranath Tagore, Indian, 1861–1941

Rocking

The divine sea rocks its
    endless waves.
Listening to the loving seas,
    I rock my child.

At night, the vagabond wind
    sways the wheat.
Listening to the loving winds,
    I rock my child.

The Heavenly Father silently rocks
    thousands of worlds.
Sensing His hand in the shadow,
    I rock my child.

Gabriela Mistral, Chilean, 1889–1957
Translated by Maria Giachetti

Amedeo Modigliani, *Gypsy Woman with Baby,* 1919

Listening to the Crows

Infant in a pinewood
Lying in a basket
Not owning anything
Not knowing
A single word

I listened to the shiny
Crows outside my window
As they spoke with one another
In a strange tribal language

And even now
When I wake up early
And overhear the crows
Calling to one another
In the cool floods of the air

The deeps of infancy
Open within me
Their wonder washes me
And instantly

My heart grows light
As light as if the world
Had never fallen.

Anne Porter, American, b. 1911

Gustav Klimt, *Baby (Cradle)*, 1917/1918

In Childhood

The first time
I saw the morning star
I was a small child
Two years old or three
I woke up sobbing

My mother came to me
Gathered me in her arms
And took me to the window
Look she said
There's the morning star

I soon gave over crying
For there it was alone
In the dawn sky
Bright and very beautiful
As beautiful as my mother.

Anne Porter, American, b. 1911

Sleep, Darling

I have a small
daughter called
Cleis, who is

like a golden
flower
    I wouldn't
take all Croesus'
kingdom with love
thrown in, for her

Sappho, Greek, 7th century BC
Translated by Mary Barnard

Berthe Morisot, *The Artist's Sister, Edma, with Her Daughter, Jeanne,* 1872

How Like an Angel Came I Down!

FROM *Wonder*

How like an angel came I down!
How bright are all things here!
When first among His works I did appear
O how their glory me did crown!
The world resembled His eternity,
In which my soul did walk;
And every thing that I did see,
Did with me talk.

The skies in their magnificence,
The lively, lovely air;
Oh how divine, how soft, how sweet, how fair!
The stars did entertain my sense,
And all the works of God so bright and pure,
So rich and great did seem,
As if they ever must endure,
In my esteem.

A native health and innocence
Within my bones did grow,
And while my God did all His glories show,
I felt a vigour in my sense
That was all spirit. I within did flow
With seas of life, like wine;
I nothing in the world did know,
But 'twas divine.

Claude Monet, *The Artist's Garden at Vétheuil*
(detail), 1880

Harsh ragged objects were conceal'd,
Oppressions, tears, and cries,
Sins, griefs, complaints, dissensions, weeping eyes,
Were hid; and only things reveal'd
Which heavenly spirits, and the angels prize.
The state of innocence
And bliss, not trades and poverties,
Did fill my sense.

The streets were pav'd with golden stones,
The boys and girls were mine.
Oh how did all their lovely faces shine!
The sons of men were holy ones.
Joy, beauty, welfare did appear to me,
And every thing which here I found,
While like an angel I did see,
Adorn'd the ground.

…

Proprieties themselves were mine,
And hedges ornaments;
Walls, boxes, coffers, and their rich contents
Did not divide my joys, but shine.
Clothes, ribbons, jewels, laces, I esteem'd
My joys by others worn;
For me they all to wear them seem'd
When I was born.

Thomas Traherne, English, 1637–1674

Pieter de Hooch, *The Bedroom*, c. 1658/1660

Nothing Is Lost

Deep in our sub-conscious, we are told
Lie all our memories, lie all the notes
Of all the music we have ever heard
And all the phrases those we loved have spoken,
Sorrows and losses time has since consoled,
Family jokes, out-moded anecdotes
Each sentimental souvenir and token
Everything seen, experienced, each word
Addressed to us in infancy, before
Before we could even know or understand
The implications of our wonderland.
There they all are, the legendary lies
The birthday treats, the sights, the sounds, the tears
Forgotten debris of forgotten years
Waiting to be recalled, waiting to rise
Before our world dissolves before our eyes
Waiting for some small, intimate reminder,
A word, a tune, a known familiar scent
An echo from the past when, innocent
We looked upon the present with delight
And doubted not the future would be kinder
And never knew the loneliness of night.

Noel Coward, English, 1899–1973

Auguste Renoir, *A Girl with a Watering Can*, 1876

Full Circle

When thou art as little as I am, Mother,
And I as old as thou,
I'll feed thee on wild-bee honeycomb,
And milk from my cow.
I'll make thee a swan's-down bed, Mother;
Watch over thee then will I.
And if in a far-away dream you start
I'll sing thee lullaby.
It's many—Oh, ages and ages, Mother,
We've shared, we two. Soon, now:
Thou shalt be happy, grown again young,
And I as old as thou.

Walter de la Mare, English, 1873–1956

Mary Cassatt, *Mother and Child* (detail), c. 1905

Emil Nolde, *Sunflowers, Pink and White Dahlias,
and a Blue Delphinium,* c. 1930/1940

When I Was Young

Often when I was young
  Gods rescued me
    From the noise and cruelty of men
     And, happy and safe, I played
      With flowers of the meadow,
       And winds of heaven
        Would play with me.

And just as you fill
Plants' hearts with joy
When they reach up
Their tender arms,

So you ravished my heart
Father Helios, and, you, blessed Luna,
Chose me, like Endymion,
For your lover!

Oh all you faithful
Benevolent Gods,
If only you knew
How my soul adored you!

At the time I could not call you by name,
And you never spoke mine
As people do, believing
They know one another.

Still, I knew you better
Than any person.
I understood the peace of the sky
But never the words of men.

I was brought up by
Whispering meadow songs,
And learned the meaning of love
Among flowers.

I grew up in the arms of gods.

Friedrich Hölderlin, German, 1770–1843
Translated by John White

Auguste Renoir, *Madame Monet and Her Son*, 1874

In the Breeze

In the breeze, Mother,
the leaves are whispering.

A small breeze is blowing
softly and lightly
moving the ship
of my thoughts;
it makes me so happy
that it seems
to bring me heaven
much too early
and the sound sends me to sleep
in the shade.

If I wake up
I wake among flowers
and barely remember
any of my troubles;
they fade away
as sleep takes me;
the rustle of leaves
gives me my life
and sends me to sleep
in the shade.

Anonymous, Spain

Those Winter Sundays

Sundays too my father got up early
and put his clothes on in the blueblack cold,
then with cracked hands that ached
from labor in the weekday weather made
banked fires blaze. No one ever thanked him.

I'd wake and hear the cold splintering, breaking.
When the rooms were warm, he'd call,
and slowly I would rise and dress,
fearing the chronic angers of that house,

Speaking indifferently to him,
who had driven out the cold
and polished my good shoes as well.
What did I know, what did I know
of love's austere and lonely offices?

Robert Hayden, American, 1913–1980

Mother to Son

Well, son, I'll tell you:
Life for me ain't been no crystal stair.
It's had tacks in it,
And splinters,
And boards torn up,
And places with no carpet on the floor—
Bare.
But all the time
I'se been a-climbin' on,
And reachin' landin's,
And turnin' corners,
And sometimes goin' in the dark
Where there ain't been no light.
So boy, don't you turn back.
Don't you set down on the steps
'Cause you finds it's kinder hard.
Don't you fall now—
For I'se still goin', honey,
I'se still climbin',
And life for me ain't been no crystal stair.

Langston Hughes, American, 1902–1967

Horace Pippin, *Interior*, 1944

Young

Before time had a name, when win
or lose were the same, in a forsaken
town I lived unnoticed, blessed.
Remember when shadows played
because there were leaves in the wind?
And people came to our door from a land
where stories were real?
Barefoot, we traveled the roads
all summer. At night we drew pictures
of home with smoke from the chimney.
And we frowned when we read,
so we could understand.

After the years came true, but before
their cost, I played in that big world, too,
and often won: this face was known;
gold came into these hands.
But unwieldy hours overwhelmed
my time. All I intended blew away.
The best of my roads went wrong,
no matter my age, no matter how long I tried.
It was far, it was dim, toward the last.
And nobody knew how heavy it was by the end,
for that same being who lived back then.

Don't you see how it was, for a child?
Don't you understand?

William Stafford, American, 1914–1993

Walker Evans, *Mount Pleasant, Pennsylvania,* 1935

Song (4)

for Guy Davenport

Within the circles of our lives
we dance the circles of the years,
the circles of the seasons
within the circles of the years,
the cycles of the moon

within the circles of the seasons,
the circles of our reasons
within the cycles of the moon.

Again, again we come and go,
changed, changing. Hands
join, unjoin in love and fear,
grief and joy. The circles turn,
each giving into each, into all.
Only music keeps us here,

each by all the others held.
In the hold of hands and eyes
we turn in pairs, that joining
joining each to all again.

And then we turn aside, alone,
out of the sunlight gone

into the darker circles of return.

Wendell Berry, American, b. 1934

Paul Gauguin, *Breton Girls Dancing, Pont-Aven*, 1888

There Was a Child Went Forth

There was a child went forth every day,
And the first object he look'd upon, that object he became,
And that object became part of him for the day or a certain
    part of the day,
Or for many years or stretching cycles of years.

The early lilacs became part of this child,
And grass and white and red morning-glories, and white and
    red clover, and the song of the phoebe-bird,
And the Third-month lambs and the sow's pink-faint litter,
    and the mare's foal and the cow's calf,
And the noisy brood of the barnyard or by the mire
    of the pondside,
And the fish suspending themselves so curiously below there,
    and the beautiful curious liquid,
And the water-plants with their graceful flat heads,
    all became part of him.

                    …

His own parents, he that had father'd him and she that had
    conceiv'd him in her womb and birth'd him,
They gave this child more of themselves than that,
They gave him afterward every day, they became part of him.

The mother at home quietly placing the dishes
    on the supper-table,
The mother with mild words, clean her cap and gown,
    a wholesome odor falling off her person and clothes
    as she walks by,
The father, strong, self-sufficient, manly, mean, anger'd, unjust,
The blow, the quick loud word, the tight bargain, the crafty lure,
The family usages, the language, the company, the furniture,
    the yearning and swelling heart,
Affection that will not be gainsay'd, the sense of what is real,
    the thought if after all it should prove unreal,
The doubts of day-time and the doubts of night-time,
    the curious whether and how,
Whether that which appears so is so, or is it all flashes
    and specks?

Walker Evans, *Subway Portrait*, 1938/1941

Men and women crowding fast in the streets, if they are not
    flashes and specks what are they?
The streets themselves and the façades of houses,
    and goods in the windows,
Vehicles, teams, the heavy-plank'd wharves, the huge crossing
    at the ferries,
The village on the highland seen from afar at sunset,
    the river between,
Shadows, aureole and mist, the light falling on roofs and gables
    of white or brown two miles off,
The schooner near by sleepily dropping down the tide,
    the little boat slack-tow'd astern,
The hurrying tumbling waves, quick-broken crests, slapping,
The strata of color'd clouds, the long bar of maroon-tint away
    solitary by itself, the spread of purity it lies motionless in,
The horizon's edge, the flying sea-crow, the fragrance
    of salt marsh and shore mud,
These became part of that child who went forth every day,
    and who now goes, and will always go forth every day.

Walt Whitman, American, 1819–1892

Jean Siméon Chardin, *Soap Bubbles*, probably 1733/1734

Sonnet

Guido, I wish that you and Lapo and I
Were carried off by magic
And put in a boat, which, every time there was wind,
Would sail on the ocean exactly where we wanted.

In this way storms and other dangerous weather
Wouldn't be able to harm us—
And I wish that, since we all were of one mind,
We would want more and more to be together.

And I wish that Vanna and Lagia too
And she whose name on the list is number thirty
Were put in the boat by the magician too

And that we all did nothing but talk about love
And I wish that they were just as glad to be there
As I believe the three of us would be.

Dante Alighieri, Italian, 1265–1321
Translated by Kenneth Koch

Winslow Homer, *Breezing Up (A Fair Wind)*, 1873–1876

A Novel

1.

One isn't serious when one is seventeen—
One fine evening—who needs beer and lemonade,
The glaring light of noisy cafes!
You stroll under green lindens along the promenade.

The lindens smell good in the good June night!
The air is so sweet, it makes you close your eyes.
The breeze full of sounds—the town isn't far—
Carries the scent of perfume and beer…

2.

Over there you notice a tiny patch
Of dark blue, framed by a little branch
Pinned up by an unruly star, that melts
With gentle shivers, small and pure white…

Night of June! Seventeen! You let yourself go.
The air is champagne and goes to your head…
The conversation wanders; you feel a kiss on your lips
Fluttering there, like an tiny insect…

3.

Your crazy Robinson Crusoe heart travels through novels,
When, in the glow of a pale streetlamp,
There passes a girl with a charming way about her
In the shadow of her father's intimidating collar.

And, since she finds you immensely naive,
With a click of her dainty boots,
She turns away at once, with a quick little twist…
Lines of old love songs die on your lips…

4.

You are in love. Busy until August.
You are in love. Your sonnets make her laugh.
All your friends abandon you; you act like a fool.
Then the adored one, one evening, deigns to write you!

That very evening—you go back to the bright cafes,
You order beer, or else, some lemonade…
One is not serious when one is seventeen
And green lindens line the promenade.

Arthur Rimbaud, French, 1854–1891

Jean-Honoré Fragonard, *The Swing*, probably c. 1765

Brown Penny

I whispered, "I am too young."
And then, "I am old enough";
Wherefore I threw a penny
To find out if I might love.
"Go and love, go and love, young man,
If the lady be young and fair."
Ah, penny, brown penny, brown penny,
I am looped in the loops of her hair.

O love is the crooked thing,
There is nobody wise enough
To find out all that is in it,
For he would be thinking of love
Till the stars had run away
And the shadows eaten the moon.
Ah, penny, brown penny, brown penny,
One cannot begin it too soon.

William Butler Yeats, Irish, 1865–1939

Bartolomé Esteban Murillo,
Two Women at a Window, c. 1655/1660

Botticelli, *Portrait of a Youth,* early 1480s

Poetry

And it was at that age…Poetry arrived
in search of me. I don't know, I don't know where
it came from, from winter or a river,
I don't know how or when,
no, they were not voices, they were not
words, nor silence,
but from a street I was summoned,
from the branches of night,
abruptly from the others,
among violent fires
or returning alone,

there I was without a face
and it touched me.

I did not know what to say, my mouth
had no way
with names,
my eyes were blind,
and something started in my soul,
fever or forgotten wings,
and I made my own way,
deciphering
that fire
and I wrote the first faint line,
faint, without substance, pure nonsense
pure wisdom
of someone who knows nothing
and suddenly I saw
the heavens unfastened
and open planets,
palpitating plantations,
shadow perforated,
riddled
with arrows, fire and flowers,
the winding night, the universe

And I, infinitesimal being,
drunk with the great starry
void,
likeness, image of
mystery,
felt myself a pure part
of the abyss,
I wheeled with the stars,
my heart broke loose on the wind.

Pablo Neruda, Chilean, 1904–1973
Translated by Alistair Reid

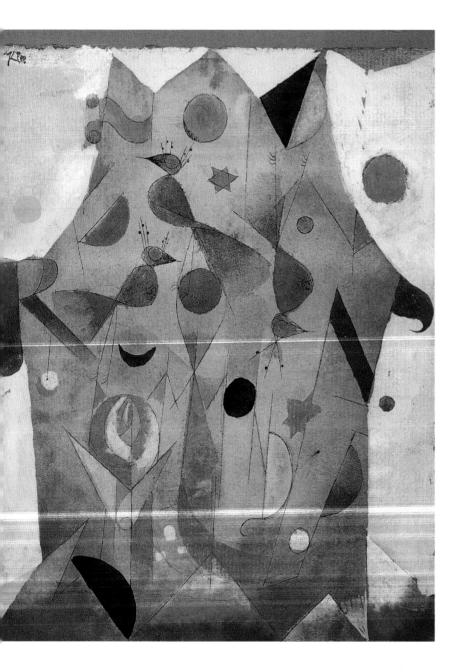

Autobiographia Literaria

When I was a child
I played by myself in a
corner of the schoolyard
all alone.

I hated dolls and I
hated games, animals were
not friendly and birds
flew away.

If anyone was looking
for me I hid behind a
tree and cried out "I am
an orphan."

And here I am, the
center of all beauty!
writing these poems!
Imagine!

Frank O'Hara, American, 1926–1966

Paul Klee, *Persische Nachtigallen*
(*Persian Nightingales*), 1917

Wishing for the Cloths of Heaven

Raphael, *Bindo Altoviti*, c. 1515

Poem for Dan's Departure

So much do we love
Talking to people we love
About ideas we love
That thinking becomes a conversation
With people we love about ideas we love.

Being your mother
Became a conversation
Where your quiet ideas furthered
The attachment first fastened
In the far configurations
Of destiny.

I am honored that the universe
Loaned your childhood to me,
Adding such a bright star
To the constellation of conversations
That I am becoming,
For, however far apart we are,
Your considerate voice stays with me,
Enlightening my thinking.

I wish I could give you
A small package of whatever I know
That is worth knowing
To take with you wherever you go.

I wish you would call me from time to time
And tell the part of me that is you
Where your part of the conversation
Is going.

Kate Farrell, American, b. 1946

Camille Pissarro, *Landscape at Les Pâtis, Pontoise,* 1868

Early One Morning

Early one morning in May I set out,
And nobody I knew was about.
    I'm bound away for ever,
      Away somewhere, away for ever.

There was no wind to trouble the weathercocks.
I had burnt my letters and darned my socks.

No one knew I was going away,
I thought myself I should come back some day.

I heard the brook through the town gardens run.
O sweet was the mud turned to dust by the sun.

A gate banged in a fence and banged in my head.
"A fine morning, sir," a shepherd said.

I could not return from my liberty,
To my youth and my love and my misery.

The past is the only dead thing that smells sweet,
The only sweet thing that is not also fleet.
    I'm bound away for ever,
      Away somewhere, away for ever.

Edward Thomas, English, 1878–1917

John Marin, *Untitled: Circus,* c. 1953

Acrobat about to Enter

Star of the bareback riding act,
Dressed in a dark-red high-collared cape,
Black-browed,
Waiting with the others
To go in:

To enter
The bright yellow
Glare of the tent,

He stood on an island,
Self-absorbed.

At twenty-one
There was trouble in his universe.

Stars were falling;
Planets made their rounds
With grating axles:

The crown of stars in blackness
Was awry.

Clouds were rising,
Thunder rumbled;
He was alone,
Nobly troubled
Waiting a moment.

He waited with challenge,
Young and in solitude,
Mourning inwardly,
Attentive to the black, fiery current
In his mind,
He would not be comforted.

Swift water,
Falling darkness:
He alone could hear it.

Hoarded the sound,
Pulled his cape around it:
Bitter and intense,
But it was his:

Youthful secret,
Black and smoldering,
Not of the crowd;

It was his private woe,
And being private,
Prized.

Robert Lax, American, b. 1915

Honoré Daumier, *Advice to a Young Artist*, probably after 1860

As Once the Wingèd Energy of Delight

As once the wingèd energy of delight
carried you over childhood's dark abysses,
now beyond your own life build the great
arch of unimagined bridges.

Wonders happen if we can succeed
in passing through the harshest danger;
but only in a bright and purely granted
achievement can we realize the wonder.

To work *with* Things in the indescribable
relationship is not too hard for us;
the pattern grows more intricate and subtle,
and being swept along is not enough.

Take your practiced powers and stretch them out
until they span the chasm between two
contradictions…For the god
wants to know himself in you.

Rainer Maria Rilke, Austrian, 1875–1926
Translated by Stephen Mitchell

Pierre Bonnard, *The Letter*, c. 1906

Hope Is the Thing with Feathers

"Hope" is the thing with feathers—
That perches in the soul—
And sings the tune without the words—
And never stops—at all—

And sweetest—in the Gale—is heard—
And sore must be the storm—
That could abash the little Bird
That kept so many warm—

I've heard it in the chillest land—
And on the strangest Sea—
Yet, never, in Extremity,
It asked a crumb—of Me.

Emily Dickinson, American, 1830–1886

Joseph Mallord William Turner, *The Dogana and Santa Maria della Salute, Venice*, 1843

Invitation to a Voyage

My darling, my dear,
Think how nice it would be
To go live there together
To love as we please
To love and to die
In a land so much like you!
The soaked suns
Of cloudy skies
Remind me of the loveliness,
So mysterious,
Of your changing eyes
Shimmering through tears

Only harmony and beauty are there,
Comfort, peace and pleasure.

Gleaming furniture
Polished by the years
Will adorn our bedroom;
Rare flowers
Will blend perfumes

With the soft scent of amber;
Soaring ceilings
Deep mirrors
Oriental splendor—
There everything will speak
Secretly to the soul
In its own private language.

Only harmony and beauty are there,
Comfort, peace and pleasure.

Those ships you see sleeping
On the canals
Are ready to sail away;
To satisfy
Your least desire is why
They came from so far away.
Setting suns
Drape the countryside
The canals, the whole city
In gold and violet
The world is falling asleep
In a warm light.

Only harmony and beauty are there,
Comfort, peace and pleasure.

Charles Baudelaire, French, 1821–1867

To the Moon

Oh gracious moon, I remember
how, a year ago, I came, in such misery,
to this same hilltop to gaze at you
and you were leaning over that forest;
just as you are now, filling it with light.
Yet, back then, your face looked
blurry and trembling through the tears
rising to my eyes, my life was
so difficult: and still is, it doesn't change,
my dearest moon. And yet it is soothing
to remember, and ponder the path
of my sorrow. Oh how we treasure,
during youth, when hope is still vast
and memory only goes a short way back,
the memories of past things,
even when sad, and the sadness is lasting

Giacomo Leopardi, Italian, 1798–1822

Waiting Both

A star looks down at me,
And says: "Here I and you
Stand each in our degree:
What do you mean to do,—
    Mean to do?"

I say: "For all I know,
Wait, and let Time go by,
Till my change come."—"Just so,"
The star says: "So mean I:—
    So mean I."

Thomas Hardy, English, 1840–1928

Italian, *Playing Cards*, 15th century

44

Julian Alden Weir, *Moonlight*, c. 1905

He Wishes for the Cloths of Heaven

Had I the heavens' embroidered cloths,
Enwrought with golden and silver light,
The blue and the dim and the dark cloths
Of night and light and the half-light,
I would spread the cloths under your feet:
But I, being poor, have only my dreams;
I have spread my dreams under your feet;
Tread softly because you tread on my dreams.

William Butler Yeats, Irish, 1865–1939

Fitz Hugh Lane, *Becalmed off Halfway Rock,* 1860

The River-Merchant's Wife: A Letter

While my hair was still cut straight across my forehead
I played about the front gate, pulling flowers.
You came by on bamboo stilts, playing horse,
You walked about my seat, playing with blue plums.
And we went on living in the village of Chōkan:
Two small people, without dislike or suspicion.

At fourteen I married My Lord you.
I never laughed, being bashful.
Lowering my head, I looked at the wall.
Called to, a thousand times, I never looked back.

At fifteen I stopped scowling,
I desired my dust to be mingled with yours
Forever and forever and forever.
Why should I climb the lookout?

At sixteen you departed,
You went into far Ku-tō-en, by the river of swirling eddies,
And you have been gone five months.
The monkeys make sorrowful noise overhead.

You dragged your feet when you went out.
By the gate now, the moss is grown, the different mosses,
Too deep to clear them away!
The leaves fall early this autumn, in wind.
The paired butterflies are already yellow with August
Over the grass in the West garden;
They hurt me. I grow older.
If you are coming down through the narrows of the river Kiang,
Please let me know beforehand,
And I will come out to meet you
    As far as Chō-fū-Sa.

Li Po, Chinese, 701–762
Translated by Ezra Pound

Albert Pinkham Ryder, *Siegfried and the Rhine Maidens*, 1888/1891

Absence

Every night I scan
the heavens with my eyes
seeking the star
that you are contemplating.

I question travelers
from the four corners of the earth
hoping to meet one
who has breathed your fragrance.

When the wind blows
I make sure it blows in my face:
the breeze might bring me
news of you.

I wander over roads
without aim, without purpose.
Perhaps a song
will sound your name.

Secretly I study
every face I see
hoping against hope
to glimpse a trace of your beauty.

Abū Bakr al-Ṭurṭūshī,
Eastern Andalusian, 1059–1126
Translated by Cola Franzen

Berthe Morisot, *The Artist's Sister at a Window*, 1869

Late Spring

Coming into the high room again after years
after oceans and shadows of hills and the sounds of lies
after losses and feet on stairs

after looking and mistakes and forgetting
turning there thinking to find
no one except those I knew
finally I saw you
sitting in white
already waiting

you of whom I had heard
with my own ears since the beginning
for whom more than once
I had opened the door
believing you were not far

W. S. Merwin, American, b. 1927

To Wait an Hour Is Long

To wait an Hour—is long—
If Love be just beyond—
To wait Eternity—is short—
If Love reward the end—

Emily Dickinson, American, 1830–1886

Titian, *Venus with a Mirror*, c. 1555

Unending Love

I seem to have loved you in numberless forms, numberless times,
In life after life, in age after age forever.
My spell-bound heart has made and re-made the necklace of songs
That you take as a gift, wear round your neck in your many forms
In life after life, in age after age forever.

Whenever I hear old chronicles of love, its age-old pain,
Its ancient tale of being apart or together,
As I stare on and on into the past, in the end you emerge
Clad in the light of a pole-star piercing the darkness of time:
You become an image of what is remembered forever.

You and I have floated here on the stream that brings from the fount
At the heart of time love of one for another.
We have played alongside millions of lovers, shared in the same
Shy sweetness of meeting, the same distressful tears of farewell—
Old love, but in shapes that renew and renew forever.

Today it is heaped at your feet, it has found its end in you,
The love of all man's days both past and forever:
Universal joy, universal sorrow, universal life,
The memories of all loves merging with this one love of ours—
And the songs of every poet past and forever.

Rabindranath Tagore, Indian, 1861–1941
Translated by William Radice

Egon Schiele, *Dancer (Die Tänzerin)*, 1913

December at Yase

You said, that October,
In the tall dry grass by the orchard
When you chose to be free,
"Again someday, maybe ten years."

After college I saw you
One time. You were strange.
And I was obsessed with a plan.

Now ten years and more have
Gone by: I've always known
     where you were—
I might have gone to you
Hoping to win your love back.
You still are single.

I didn't.
I thought I must make it alone. I
Have done that.

Only in dream, like this dawn,
Does the grave, awed intensity
Of our young love
Return to my mind, to my flesh.

We had what the others
All crave and seek for;
We left it behind at nineteen.

I feel ancient, as though I had
Lived many lives.

And may never now know
If I am a fool
Or have done what my
     karma demands.

Gary Snyder, American, b. 1930

The Road Not Taken

Two roads diverged in a yellow wood,
And sorry I could not travel both
And be one traveler, long I stood
And looked down one as far as I could
To where it bent in the undergrowth;

Then took the other, as just as fair,
And having perhaps the better claim,
Because it was grassy and wanted wear;
Though as for that, the passing there
Had worn them really about the same,

And both that morning equally lay
In leaves no step had trodden black.
Oh, I kept the first for another day!
Yet knowing how way leads on to way,
I doubted if I should ever come back.

I shall be telling this with a sigh
Somewhere ages and ages hence:
Two roads diverged in a wood, and I—
I took the one less traveled by,
And that has made all the difference.

Robert Frost, American, 1874–1963

Paul Cézanne, *Bend in the Road*, 1900–1906

Alfred Sisley, *The Road in the Woods*, 1879

Come, Let Us Find

Come, let us find a cottage, love,
  That's green for half a mile around;
To laugh at every grumbling bee,
  Whose sweetest blossom's not yet found.
Where many a bird shall sing for you,
  And in our garden build its nest:
They'll sing for you as though their eggs
  Were lying in your breast,
    My love—
  Were lying warm in your soft breast.

'Tis strange how men find time to hate,
  When Life is all too short for love;
But we, away from our own kind,
  A different life can live and prove.
And early on a summer's morn,
  As I go walking out with you,
We'll help the sun with our warm breath
  To clear away the dew,
    My love,
  To clear away the morning dew.

William H. Davies, English, 1870–1940

Auguste Renoir, *Picking Flowers*, 1875

What Wondrous Life Is This I Lead!

FROM *The Garden*

What wondrous life is this I lead!
Ripe apples drop about my head;
The luscious clusters of the vine
Upon my mouth do crush their wine;
The nectarine and curious peach
Into my hands themselves do reach;
Stumbling on melons, as I pass,
Ensnared with flowers, I fall on grass.

Meanwhile the mind, from pleasure less,
Withdraws into its happiness;
The mind, that ocean where each kind
Does straight its own resemblance find;
Yet it creates, transcending these,
Far other worlds and other seas,
Annihilating all that's made
To a green thought in a green shade.

Here at the fountain's sliding foot
Or at some fruit-tree's mossy root,
Casting the body's vest aside
My soul into the boughs does glide:
There, like a bird, it sits and sings,
Then whets and claps its silver wings,
And, till prepared for longer flight,
Waves in its plumes the various light.

Andrew Marvell, English, 1621–1678

55

Jean-Baptiste-Camille Corot, *Ville d'Avray*, c. 1867/1870

The Happiest Day

It was early May, I think
a moment of lilac or dogwood
when so many promises are made
it hardly matters if a few are broken.
My mother and father still hovered
in the background, part of the scenery
like the houses I had grown up in,
and if they would be torn down later
that was something I knew
but didn't believe. Our children were asleep
or playing, the youngest as new
as the new smell of the lilacs,
and how could I have guessed
their roots were shallow
and would be easily transplanted.
I didn't even guess that I was happy.
The small irritations that are like salt
on melon were what I dwelt on,
though in truth they simply
made the fruit taste sweeter.
So we sat on the porch
in the cool morning, sipping
hot coffee. Behind the news of the day —

strikes and small wars, a fire somewhere—
I could see the top of your dark head
and thought not of public conflagrations
but of how it would feel on my bare shoulder.
If someone could stop the camera then…
if someone could only stop the camera
and ask me: are you happy?
perhaps I would have noticed
how the morning shone in the reflected
color of lilac. Yes, I might have said
and offered a steaming cup of coffee.

Linda Pastan, American, b. 1932

The Moment

To write down all I contain at this moment
I would pour the desert through an hour-glass,
The sea through a water-clock,
Grain by grain and drop by drop
Let in the trackless, measureless, mutable seas and sands.

For earth's days and nights are breaking over me,
The tides and sands are running through me,
And I have only two hands and a heart to hold the desert and the sea.

What can I contain of it? It escapes and eludes me,
The tides wash me away,
The desert shifts under my feet.

Kathleen Raine, English, b. 1908

Johannes Vermeer, *A Lady Writing*, c. 1665

Mary Cassatt, *The Boating Party*, 1893/1894

Song

What are days?
We are all days
My friend
We are all life
My love
We love and we live
We live and we love
And we do not know what life is
And we do not know what day is
And we do not know what love is.

Jacques Prevert, French, 1900–1977
Translated by Harriet Zinnes

Priceless Gifts

An empty day without events.
And that is why
it grew immense
as space. And suddenly
happiness of being
entered me.

I heard
in my heartbeat
the birth of time
and each instant of life
one after the other
came rushing in
like priceless gifts.

Anna Swir, Polish, 1909–1984
Translated by Czeslaw Milosz and
Leonard Nathan

In This Short Life

In this short Life
That only lasts an hour
How much—how little—is
Within our power.

Emily Dickinson,
American, 1830–1886

Claude Monet, *Woman with
a Parasol—Madame Monet
and Her Son*, 1875

Edouard Manet, *The Railway,* 1873

Why the Face of the Clock Is Not Truly a Circle

Time is not gone,
Time does not go,
Time can be found again
Old men know
If you travel a journey.

Paris again
And that scent in the air,
That sound in the street,
And the time is still there
At the end of the journey.

Turn at the door
Climb the stone stair—
What fragrance is that
In the dark, on the air,
At the end of the journey?

Time does not go:
Time keeps its place.
But oh the brown hair
And oh the bright face!
Where? By what journey?

Archibald MacLeish, American,
1892–1982

Berthe Morisot, *The Mother and Sister of the Artist*, 1869/1870

Mother and Me

Pretty soon I shall be the same age as my mother
maybe I'll even get to be as old as her in suffering
then we'll be able to talk at last
woman to woman and I'll not
ask her stupid questions
not because I know too much
but because there's no answer
and we shan't argue any more
about God or Poland
true understanding
is always silence

Anna Kamienska, Polish, 1920–1986
Translated by Krzysztof Piechowicz and Daniel Weissbort

Thomas Cole, *Sunrise in the Catskills,* 1826

I Know I Have the Best of Time and Space

FROM *Song of Myself*

I know I have the best of time and space, and was
    never measured and never will be measured.

I tramp a perpetual journey, (come listen all!)
My signs are a rain-proof coat, good shoes, and
    a staff cut from the woods,
No friend of mine takes his ease in my chair,
I have no chair, no church, no philosophy,
I lead no man to a dinner-table, library, exchange,
But each man and each woman of you I lead
    upon a knoll,
My left hand hooking you round the waist,
My right hand pointing to landscapes of continents
    and the public road.

Not I, not any one else can travel that road for you,
You must travel it for yourself.

It is not far, it is within reach,
Perhaps you have been on it since you were born
    and did not know,
Perhaps it is everywhere on water and on land.

Shoulder your duds dear son, and I will mine,
    and let us hasten forth,
Wonderful cities and free nations we shall fetch
    as we go.

If you tire, give me both burdens, and rest
    the chuff of your hand on my hip,
And in due time you shall repay the same service to me,
For after we start we never lie by again.

This day before dawn I ascended a hill and look'd
    at the crowded heaven,
And I said to my spirit *When we become the enfolders*
    of those orbs, and the pleasure and knowledge of every
    thing in them, shall we be fill'd and satisfied then?
And my spirit said *No, we but level that lift to pass*
    and continue beyond.

You are also asking me questions and I hear you,
I answer that I cannot answer, you must find out
    for yourself.

Sit a while dear son,
Here are biscuits to eat and here is milk to drink,
But as soon as you sleep and renew yourself in
    sweet clothes, I kiss you with a good-by kiss
    and open the gate for your egress hence.

Long enough have you dream'd contemptible
    dreams,
Now I wash the gum from your eyes,
You must habit yourself to the dazzle of the light
    and of every moment of your life.

Long have you timidly waded holding a plank
    by the shore,
Now I will you to be a bold swimmer,
To jump off in the midst of the sea, rise again, nod
    to me, shout, and laughingly dash with your hair.

Walt Whitman, American, 1819–1892

Midway through the Journey

Florentine, *Allegorical Portrait of Dante,* late 16th century

Midway through the Journey

FROM *The Divine Comedy*

Midway through the journey of our life
    I found myself in a dark forest
    with the right path nowhere in sight.
Oh how hard to say what it was like,
    that savage forest, so rugged and brutal
    that the very thought brings back my fright!
Death can hardly have more horror,
    but in order to relate the good I found there,
    I will say what else I encountered.
I am still not sure how I got there,
    so full of sleep was I at the moment
    when I abandoned the true path.
But once I reached the foot of the hill
    rising at the end of the valley
    which had stricken my heart with such fear,
I looked up and saw the hill's shoulders
    cloaked with the rays of that planet
    which leads people straight down every road.
This somewhat calmed the terror
    the lake of my heart had endured
    all night long with such misery,
And like someone who, panting for breath,
    after escaping from sea to shore
    turns to see the perilous waters left behind,
So did my soul, still in flight,
    turn back to gaze again at the pass
    through which no one else had ever come alive.

Dante Alighieri, Italian, 1265–1321

To Be or Not To Be

FROM *Hamlet*

To be, or not to be: that is the question:
Whether 'tis nobler in the mind to suffer
The slings and arrows of outrageous fortune,
Or to take arms against a sea of troubles,
And by opposing end them? To die: to sleep;
No more; and, by a sleep to say we end
The heart-ache and the thousand natural shocks
That flesh is heir to, 'tis a consummation
Devoutly to be wish'd. To die, to sleep;
To sleep: perchance to dream: ay, there's the rub;
For in that sleep of death what dreams may come
When we have shuffled off this mortal coil,
Must give us pause. There's the respect
That makes calamity of so long life;
For who would bear the whips and scorns of time,
The oppressor's wrong, the proud man's contumely,
The pangs of dispriz'd love, the law's delay,
The insolence of office, and the spurns
That patient merit of the unworthy takes,
When he himself might his quietus make
With a bare bodkin? Who would fardels bear,
To grunt and sweat under a weary life,
But that the dread of something after death,
The undiscover'd country from whose bourn
No traveler returns, puzzles the will,
And makes us rather bear those ills we have
Than fly to others that we know not of?

Edouard Manet, *The Tragic Actor*
(*Rouvière as Hamlet*), 1866

Thus conscience does make cowards of us all;
And thus the native hue of resolution
Is sicklied o'er with the pale cast of thought,
And enterprises of great pitch and moment
With this regard their currents turn awry,
And lose the name of action.

William Shakespeare, English, 1564–1616

Mirage

The hope I dreamed of was a dream,
    Was but a dream; and now I wake,
Exceeding comfortless, and worn, and old,
    For a dream's sake.

I hang my harp upon a tree,
    A weeping willow in a lake;
I hang my silenced harp there, wrung and snapt
    For a dream's sake.

Lie still, lie still, my breaking heart;
    My silent heart, lie still and break:
Life, and the world, and mine own self are changed
    For a dream's sake.

Christina Rossetti, English, 1830–1894

We Never Said Farewell

We never said farewell, nor even looked
    Our last upon each other, for no sign
Was made when we the linkèd chain unhooked
    And broke the level line.

And here we dwell together, side by side,
    Our places fixed for life upon the chart.
Two islands that the roaring seas divide
    Are not more far apart.

Mary Coleridge, English, 1861–1907

Men at Forty

Men at forty
Learn to close softly
The doors to rooms they will not be
Coming back to.

At rest on a stair landing,
They feel it
Moving beneath them now
    like the deck of a ship,
Though the swell is gentle.

And deep in mirrors
They rediscover
The face of the boy as he practices tying
His father's tie there in secret

And the face of that father,
Still warm with the mystery of lather.
They are more fathers than
    sons themselves now.
Something is filling them, something

That is like the twilight sound
Of the crickets, immense,
Filling the woods at the foot of the slope
Behind their mortgaged houses.

Donald Justice, American, b. 1925

Edward Hopper, *Cape Cod Evening* (detail), 1939

Tonight I Can Write

Tonight I can write the saddest lines.

Write, for example, "The night is shattered
and the blue stars shiver in the distance."

The night wind revolves in the sky and sings.

Tonight I can write the saddest lines.
I loved her, and sometimes she loved me too.

Through nights like this one I held her in my arms.
I kissed her again and again under the endless sky.

She loved me, sometimes I loved her too.
How could one not have loved her great still eyes.

Tonight I can write the saddest lines.
To think that I do not have her. To feel that I have lost her.

To hear the immense night, still more immense without her.
And the verse falls to the soul like dew to the pasture.

What does it matter that my love could not keep her.
The night is shattered and she is not with me.

This is all. In the distance someone is singing. In the distance.
My soul is not satisfied that it has lost her.

My sight searches for her as though to go to her.
My heart looks for her, and she is not with me.

The same night whitening the same trees.
We, of that time, are no longer the same.

I no longer love her, that's certain, but how I loved her.
My voice tried to find the wind to touch her hearing.

Another's. She will be another's. Like my kisses before.
Her voice. Her bright body. Her infinite eyes.

I no longer love her, that's certain, but maybe I love her.
Love is so short, forgetting is so long.

Because through nights like this one I held her in my arms
my soul is not satisfied that it has lost her.

Though this be the last pain that she makes me suffer
and these the last verses that I write for her.

Pablo Neruda, Chilean, 1904–1973
Translated by W. S. Merwin

In Our Souls

    In our souls everything
moves guided by a mysterious hand.
We know nothing of our own souls
that are ununderstandable and say nothing.

    The deepest words
of the wise man teach us
the same as the whistle of the wind when it blows
or the sound of the water when it is flowing.

Antonio Machado, Spanish, 1875–1939
Translated by Robert Bly

Henry Ossawa Tanner, *The Seine* (detail), c. 1902

Paul Klee, *New House in the Suburbs*, 1924

The Sky over My Mother's House

It is a July night
scented with gardenias.
The moon and stars shine
hiding the essence of the night.
As darkness fell
—with its deepening onyx shadows
and the golden brilliance of the stars—
my mother put the garden, her house,
    the kitchen, in order.
Now, as she sleeps,
I walk in her garden
immersed in the solitude of the moment.
I have forgotten the names
of many trees and flowers
and there used to be more pines
where orange trees flower now.
Tonight I think of all the skies
I have pondered and once loved.
Tonight the shadows around
the house are kind.
The sky is a camera obscura
projecting blurred images.
In my mother's house
the twinkling stars
pierce me with nostalgia,
and each thread in the net that
    surrounds this world
is a wound that will not heal.

Jaime Manrique, American, b. Colombia, 1949
Translated by Edith Grossman

James Rosenquist, *Welcome to the Water Planet*, 1987

I Ask My Mother to Sing

She begins, and my grandmother joins her.
Mother and daughter sing like young girls.
If my father were alive, he would play
his accordion and sway like a boat.

I've never been in Peking, or the Summer Palace,
nor stood on the great Stone Boat to watch
the rain begin on Kuen Ming Lake, the picnickers
running away in the grass.

But I love to hear it sung;
how the waterlilies fill with rain until
they overturn, spilling water into water,
then rock back, and fill with more.

Both women have begun to cry.
But neither stops her song.

Li-Young Lee, American, b. 1957

René Magritte, *La condition humaine*, 1933

At a Window

Give me hunger,
O you gods that sit and give
The world its orders.
Give me hunger, pain and want,
Shut me out with shame and failure
From your doors of gold and fame,
Give me your shabbiest, weariest hunger!

But leave me a little love,
A voice to speak to me in the day end,
A hand to touch me in the dark room
Breaking the long loneliness.
In the dusk of day-shapes
Blurring the sunset,
One little wandering, western star
Thrust out from the changing shores of shadow.
Let me go to the window,
Watch there the day-shapes of dusk
And wait and know the coming
Of a little love.

Carl Sandburg, American, 1878–1967

At the Beach

Footprints that met in the sand were erased.
The people who left them were erased as well
by the wind of their being no more.

The few became many and the many will be
    without end
like the sand on the seashore. I found an envelope
with an address on the front and the back.
But inside it was empty and silent. The letter
was read somewhere else, like a soul that left the body.

That happy melody in the big white house last night
is now full of longing and full of sand
like the bathing suits hanging on a line between
    the wooden poles.

Water birds shriek when they see land
and people when they see tranquillity.
Oh my children, children of my mind
that I made with all my body and all my soul,
now they are only the children of my mind
and I am alone on this beach
with the low shivering grasses of the dunes.
That shiver is their language. That shiver
is my language.
We have a common language.

Yehuda Amichai, Israeli, b. 1924

Malcolm Morley, *Rite of Passage*, published 1988

Edvard Munch, *Two Women
on the Shore (Frauen am
Meeresufer)*, c. 1898

To That Which Is Most Important

Were I able to shut
my eyes, ears, legs, hands
and walk into myself
for a thousand years,
perhaps I would reach
—I do not know its name—
what matters most.

Anna Swir, Polish, 1909–1984
Translated by Czeslaw Milosz and Leonard Nathan

Beach Sandals

I swam away from myself.
Do not call me.
Swim away from yourself, too.

We will swim away, leaving our bodies
on the shore
like a pair of beach sandals.

Anna Swir, Polish, 1909–1984
Translated by Czeslaw Milosz and Leonard Nathan

William Blake, *The Great Red Dragon and the Woman Clothed with the Sun*, c. 1805

I Fell

I fell
because of wisdom,
but was not destroyed:
through her I dived
into the great sea,
and in those depths
I seized
a wealth-bestowing pearl.

I descended
like the great iron anchor
men use to steady their ships
in the night on rough seas,
and holding up the bright lamp
that I there received,
I climbed the rope
to the boat of understanding.

While in the dark sea,
I slept,
and not overwhelmed there,
dreamt: a star
blazed in my womb.

I marveled
at that light,
and grasped it,
and brought it up to the sun.
I laid hold upon it,
and will not let it go.

Makeda, Queen of Sheba,
Ethiopian, c. 1000 BC
Translated by Jane Hirshfield

Rembrandt van Rijn, *The Mill*, 1645/1648

In a Dark Time

In a dark time, the eye begins to see,
I meet my shadow in the deepening shade;
I hear my echo in the echoing wood —
A lord of nature weeping to a tree.
I live between the heron and the wren,
Beasts of the hill and serpents of the den.

What's madness but nobility of soul
At odds with circumstance? The day's on fire!
I know the purity of pure despair,
My shadow pinned against a sweating wall.
That place among the rocks — is it a cave,
Or a winding path? The edge is what I have.

A steady stream of correspondences!
A night flowing with birds, a ragged moon,
And in broad day the midnight come again!
A man goes far to find out what he is —
Death of the self in a long, tearless night,
All natural shapes blazing unnatural light.

Dark, dark my light, and darker my desire.
My soul, like some heat-maddened summer fly,
Keeps buzzing at the sill. Which I is I?
A fallen man, I climb out of my fear.
The mind enters itself, and God the mind,
And one is One, freeing in the tearing wind.

Theodore Roethke, American, 1908–1963

Georges de La Tour, *The Repentant Magdalene*, c. 1640

The Holy Longing

Tell a wise person, or else keep silent,
Because the massman will mock it right away.
I praise what is truly alive,
What longs to be burned to death.

In the calm water of the love-nights,
Where you were begotten, where you have begotten,
A strange feeling comes over you
When you see the silent candle burning.

Now you are no longer caught
In the obsession with darkness,
And a desire for higher love-making
Sweeps you upward.

Distance does not make you falter,
Now, arriving in magic, flying,
And, finally, insane for the light,
You are the butterfly and you are gone.

And so long as you haven't experienced
This: to die and so to grow,
You are only a troubled guest
On the dark earth.

Johann Wolfgang von Goethe, German, 1749–1832
Translated by Robert Bly

Ludolf Bakhuysen, *Ships in Distress off a Rocky Coast*, 1667

The Pulley

When God at first made man,
Having a glass of blessings standing by—
"Let us" (said he) "pour on him all we can;
Let the world's riches, which dispersed lie,
    Contract into a span."

So strength first made a way;
Then beauty flowed, then wisdom, honor, pleasure.
When almost all was out, God made a stay,
Perceiving that alone of all his treasure
    Rest in the bottom lay.

"For if I should" (said he)
"Bestow this jewel also on my creature,
He would adore my gifts instead of me,
And rest in Nature, not the God of Nature;
    So both should losers be.

Yet let him keep the rest,
But keep them with repining restlessness.
Let him be rich and weary, that at least,
If goodness lead him not, yet weariness
    May toss him to my breast."

George Herbert, English, 1593–1633

Georges Seurat, *Seascape at Port-en-Bessin, Normandy,* 1888

How Serene the Life

FROM *A Life Apart*

How serene the life of someone
who flees worldly clamor
and follows the hidden path
chosen by those few
wise ones of the world!

For his heart is not dazed
by magnificent ways,
nor is he dazzled
by ingenious golden domes
atop jasper columns.

He does not wait for fame
to eagerly sing his name;
nor does he have to hear
flattering tongues praise
what plain truth blames.

What joy would it bring me
to see vain fingers point at me?
To breathlessly chase
the wind of glory
with burning longing, with withering worry?

Oh, mountain! Oh, meadow! Oh, clear stream!
Oh, hiding place, safe and delightful!
In my storm-battered ship
Let me flee these treacherous seas
To your dear peace.

Fray Luis de Leon, Spanish, 1527–1591

Demand

Listen!
Dear dream of utter aliveness—
Touching my body of utter death—
Tell me, O quickly! dream of aliveness,
The flaming source of your bright breath.
Tell me, O dream of utter aliveness—
Knowing so well the wind and the sun—
    Where is this light
    Your eyes see forever?
    And what is this wind
    You touch when you run?

Langston Hughes, American, 1902–1967

Vincent van Gogh, *Farmhouse in Provence*, 1888

Lilies

I have been thinking
about living
like the lilies
that blow in the fields.

They rise and fall
in the wedge of the wind,
and have no shelter
from the tongues of the cattle,

and have no closets or cupboards,
and have no legs.
Still I would like to be
as wonderful

as that old idea.
But if I were a lily
I think I would wait all day
for the green face

of the hummingbird
to touch me.
What I mean is,
could I forget myself

even in those feathery fields?
When van Gogh
preached to the poor
of course he wanted to save someone—

most of all himself.
He wasn't a lily,
and wandering through the bright fields
only gave him more ideas

it would take his life to solve.
I think I will always be lonely
in this world, where the cattle
graze like a black and white river—

where the ravishing lilies
melt, without protest, on their tongues—
where the hummingbird, whenever there is a fuss,
just rises and floats away

Mary Oliver, American, b. 1935

And the Days Are Not Full Enough

And the days are not full enough
And the nights are not full enough
And life slips by like a field mouse
    Not shaking the grass.

Ezra Pound, American, 1885–1972

Joseph Mallord William Turner, *Keelmen Heaving in Coals by Moonlight,* 1835

Dover Beach

The sea is calm tonight,
The tide is full, the moon lies fair
Upon the straits;—on the French coast the light
Gleams and is gone; the cliffs of England stand,
Glimmering and vast, out in the tranquil bay.
Come to the window, sweet is the night-air!

Only, from the long line of spray
Where the sea meets the moon-blanched land,
Listen! you hear the grating roar
Of pebbles which the waves draw back, and fling,
At their return, up the high strand,
Begin, and cease, and then again begin,
With tremulous cadence slow, and bring
The eternal note of sadness in.

Sophocles long ago
Heard it on the Aegean, and it brought
Into his mind the turbid ebb and flow
Of human misery; we
Find also in the sound a thought,
Hearing it by this distant northern sea.

The Sea of Faith
Was once, too, at the full, and round earth's shore
Lay like the folds of a bright girdle furled.
But now I only hear
Its melancholy, long, withdrawing roar,
Retreating, to the breath
Of the night-wind, down the vast edges drear
And naked shingles of the world.

Ah, love, let us be true
To one another! for the world, which seems
To lie before us like a land of dreams,
So various, so beautiful, so new,
Hath really neither joy, nor love, nor light.
Nor certitude, nor peace, nor help for pain;
And we are here as on a darkling plain
Swept with confused alarms of struggle and flight,
Where ignorant armies clash by night.

Matthew Arnold, English, 1822–1888

Oceans

I have a feeling that my boat
Has struck, down there in the depths,
against a great thing.
            And nothing
happens! Nothing…Silence…Waves…

—Nothing happens? Or has everything happened,
and are we standing now, quietly, in the new life?

Juan Ramón Jiménez, Spanish, 1898–1936
Translated by Robert Bly

Henri Matisse, *La Coiffure,* 1901

Love Song

Sweep the house clean,
hang fresh curtains
in the windows
put on a new dress
and come with me!
The elm is scattering
its little loaves
of sweet smells
from a white sky!

Who shall hear of us
in the time to come?
Let him say there was
a burst of fragrance
from black branches.

William Carlos Williams, American, 1883–1963

A Little Heartsong

You came suddenly into my heart
Let me beg to live in yours
Lonely, I walked life's path
Until you undertook to draw me
Into other roads, which led into a garden
Where you live in endless beauty.

James Laughlin, American, b. 1914

Claude Monet, *The Artist's Garden in Argenteuil* (detail), 1873

Marsden Hartley, *Mount Katahdin, Maine,* 1942

The Song Turning Back into Itself 6

terrestrial blues

Again
who am I?
Certainly not the boy
I started out to be
nor the man
nor the poet

Sometimes
alone & saddened
(which is to say joyous)
I get glimpses of myself
the eternal spirit
floating from flower
to tree to grasshopper,
thru whole herds of cattle

I become the skies,
the very air itself—
Me: all things
Me: nothing

It would confuse me
if I didnt know
these lbs. of meat
bearing the name
my people gave me
to be simply
every body's condition

My soul
knows no name,
no home in being

My soul
seeks your soul

Let us laugh
each at the other
& be friends

Al Young, American, b. 1939

Your Life

Your life is like
 the high sigh
  of the breeze blowing
   through the pines

and all in all
 all is well
  well being
   here among the pines
   at Sumiyoshi.

Ryonyin-hisho, Japanese, 12th century
Translated by Yasuhiko Moriguchi and David Jenkins

Hiroshige, *Bird on a Tree*

Sonnet XXIX

When in disgrace with fortune and men's eyes
I all alone beweep my outcast state,
And trouble deaf heaven with my bootless cries,
And look upon myself and curse my fate,
Wishing me like to one more rich in hope,
Featured like him, like him with friends possessed,
Desiring this man's art, and that man's scope,
With what I most enjoy contented least;
Yet in these thoughts myself almost despising,
Haply I think on thee—and then my state,
Like to the lark at break of day arising
From sullen earth, sings hymns at heaven's gate;
  For thy sweet love remembered, such wealth brings
  That then I scorn to change my state with kings.

William Shakespeare, English, 1564–1616

Love's Maturity

In the beginning Love satisfies us.
When Love first spoke to me of love—
How I laughed at her in return!
But then she made me like the hazel trees,
Which blossom early in the season of darkness,
And bear fruit slowly.

Hadewijch of Antwerp, Flemish, 13th century
Translated by Oliver Davies

A Man and a Woman Sit Near Each Other

A man and a woman sit near each other, and they do not long
at this moment to be older, or younger, nor born
in any other nation, or time, or place.
They are content to be where they are, talking or not-talking.
Their breaths together feed someone whom we do not know.
The man sees the way his fingers move;
he sees her hands close around a book she hands to him.
They obey a third body that they share in common.
They have made a promise to love that body.
Age may come, parting may come, death will come.
A man and a woman sit near each other;
as they breathe they feed someone we do not know,
someone we know of, whom we have never seen.

Robert Bly, American, b. 1926

Edouard Vuillard, *Repast in a Garden* (detail), 1898

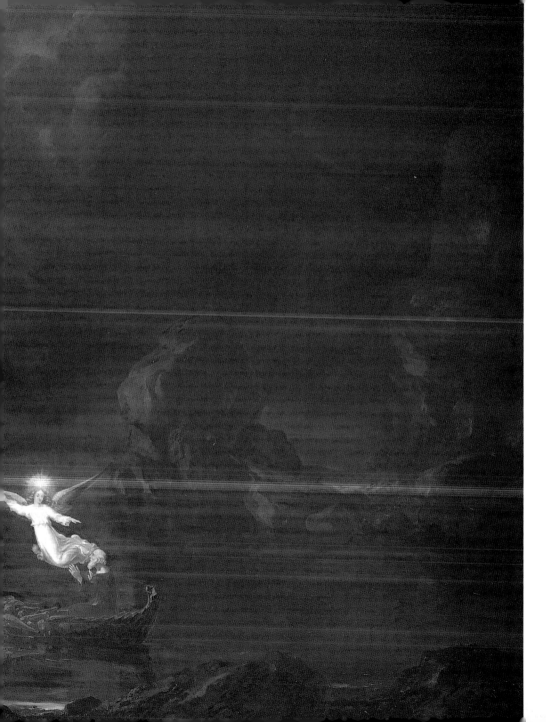

In Age I Bud Again

I Return to the Place I Was Born

From my youth up I never liked the city.
I never forgot the mountains where I was born.
The world caught me and harnessed me
And drove me through dust, thirty years away from home.
Migratory birds return to the same tree.
Fish find their way back to the pools where they were hatched.

I have been over the whole country,
And have come back at last to the garden of my childhood.

My farm is only ten acres.
The farm house has eight or nine rooms.
Elms and willows shade the back garden.
Peach trees stand by the front door.
The village is out of sight.
You can hear dogs bark in the alleys,
And cocks crow in the mulberry trees.
When you come through the gate into the court
You will find no dust or mess.
Peace and quiet live in every room.
I am content to stay here the rest of my life.
At last I have found myself.

Tao Yuan Ming (Tao Qian), Chinese, 365–427

Qing Dynasty, *Rectangular Vase Illustrating Poems by Tao Qian and Su Shi*, 1662 /1722

Henri Matisse, *Pot of Geraniums*, 1912

In Age I Bud Again

FROM *The Flower*

Who would have thought my shriveled heart
Could have recovered greenness? It was gone
    Quite under ground, as flowers depart
To feed their mother-root when they have blown,
        Where they together
        All the hard weather
    Dead to the world, keep house unknown.

These are thy wonders, Lord of Power,
Killing and quickening, bringing down to hell
    And up to heaven in an hour;
Making a chiming of a passing-bell.
        We say amiss,
        This or that is:
    Thy word is all, if we could spell.

        …

And now in age I bud again,
After so many deaths I live and write;
    I once more smell the dew and rain,
And relish versing: O my only Light,
        It cannot be
        That I am he
    On whom thy tempests fell all night.

George Herbert, English, 1593–1633

The House of Gathering

If old age is a house of gathering,
Then the hands are full.
There are old trees to prune
And young plants to plant,
There are seeds to be sown.
Not less of anything
But more of everything
To care for,
To maintain,
To keep sorted out,
A profusion of people
To answer, to respond to.

But we have been ripening
To a greater ease,
Learning to accept
That all hungers cannot be fed,
That saving the world
May be a matter
Of sowing a seed
Not overturning a tyrant,
That we do what we can.

The moment of vision,
The seizure still makes
Its relentless demands:

Work, love, be silent.
Speak.

May Sarton, American, 1912–1995

Camille Pissarro, *The Artist's Garden at Eragny*, 1898

Answers

If I envy anyone it must be
My grandmother in a long ago
Green summer, who hurried
Between kitchen and orchard on small
Uneducated feet, and took easily
All shining fruits into her eager hands.

That summer I hurried too, wakened
To books and music and circling philosophies.
I sat in the kitchen sorting through volumes of answers
That could not solve the mystery of the trees.

My grandmother stood among her kettles and ladles.
Smiling, in faulty grammar,
She praised my fortune and urged my lofty career.
So to please her I studied—but I will remember always
How she poured confusion out, how she cooled and labeled
All the wild sauces of the brimming year.

Mary Oliver, American, b. 1935

My Life Has Been the Poem I Would Have Writ

My life has been the poem I would have writ,
But I could not both live and utter it.

Henry David Thoreau, American, 1817-1862

To Everything There Is a Season

To everything there is a season, and a time
    to every purpose under the heaven:
A time to be born, and a time to die; a time
    to plant, and a time to pluck up that
    which is planted;
A time to kill and a time to heal; a time to
    break down, and a time to build up;
A time to weep, and a time to laugh; a time
    to mourn, and a time to dance;
A time to cast away stones, and a time to
    gather stones together; a time to embrace,
    and a time to refrain from embracing;
A time to get, and a time to lose; a time to
    keep and a time to cast away;
A time to rend, and a time to sew; a time to
    keep silence, and a time to speak;
A time to love, and a time to hate; a time of
    war, and a time of peace.
What profit hath he that worketh in that
    wherein he laboreth?
I have seen the travail, which God hath given
    to the sons of men to be exercised in it.
He hath made everything beautiful in his time:
    also he hath set the world in their heart,
so that no man can find out the work that
    God maketh from the beginning to the end.

Ecclesiastes 3:1–11

The Lesson of the Falling Leaves

the leaves believe
such letting go is love
such love is faith
such faith is grace
such grace is god
i agree with the leaves

Lucille Clifton, American, b. 1936

Paul Cézanne, *Still Life*, c. 1900

Jasper Francis Cropsey, *Autumn — On the Hudson River,* 1860

Sonnet LXXIII

That time of year thou mayst in me behold,
When yellow leaves, or none, or few, do hang
Upon those boughs which shake against the cold,
Bare ruined choirs, where late the sweet birds sang.
In me thou seest the twilight of such day,
As after sunset fadeth in the west,
Which by and by black night doth take away,
Death's second self, that seals up all in rest.

In me thou seest the glowing of such fire,
That on the ashes of his youth doth lie,
As the death-bed whereon it must expire,
Consumed with that which it was nourished by.
    This thou perceiv'st, which makes thy love more strong,
    To love that well which thou must leave ere long.

William Shakespeare, English, 1564–1616

Otherwise

I got out of bed
on two strong legs.
It might have been
otherwise. I ate
cereal, sweet
milk, ripe, flawless
peach. It might
have been otherwise.
I took the dog uphill
to the birch wood.
All morning I did
the work I love.

At noon I lay down
with my mate. It might
have been otherwise.
We ate dinner together
at a table with silver
candlesticks. It might
have been otherwise.
I slept in a bed
in a room with paintings
on the walls, and
planned another day
just like this day.
But one day, I know,
it will be otherwise.

Jane Kenyon, American, b. 1947

Edouard Manet, *Flowers in a Crystal Vase*, c. 1882
Opposite: Edouard Manet, *Still Life with Melon and Peaches*, c. 1866

Thanks in Old Age

Thanks in old age—thanks ere I go,
For health, the midday sun, the impalpable air—for life,
    mere life,
For precious ever-lingering memories (of you my mother
    dear—you, father—you, brothers, sisters, friends)
For all my days—not those of peace alone—the days
    of war the same,
For gentle words, caresses, gifts from foreign lands,
For shelter, wine and meat—for sweet appreciation,
(You distant, dim unknown—or young or old—countless,
    unspecified, readers belov'd,
We never met, and ne'er shall meet—and yet our souls
    embrace, long, close and long)
For beings, groups, love, deeds, words, books—for
    colors, forms,
For all the brave strong men—devoted, hardy men—who've
    forward sprung in freedom's help, all years, all lands,
For braver, stronger, more devoted men—(a special laurel
    ere I go, to life's war's chosen ones,
The cannoneers of song and thought—the great artillerists—
    the foremost leaders, captains of the soul)
As soldier from an ended war return'd—As traveler out of
    myriads, to the long procession retrospective,
Thanks—joyful thanks!—a soldier's, traveler's thanks.

Walt Whitman, American, 1819–1892

Qing Dynasty, *Shou Lao, The God of Longevity,* 1662–1722

The Ticket

On the night table
Beside my bed
I keep a small
Blue ticket

One day I found it
In my pocket-book
I don't know how
It got there

I don't know
What it's for

On one side
There's a number
98833
And
INDIANA TICKET COMPANY

And on the other side
The only thing it says
Is KEEP THIS TICKET

I keep it carefully
Because I'm old
Which means
I'll soon be leaving
For another country

Where possibly
Some blinding-bright
Enormous angel

Will stop me
At the border

And ask
To see my ticket.

Anne Porter, American, b. 1911

Lucille Chabot, *Gabriel
Weather Vane*, c. 1939

Pierre Bonnard,
The Bath (detail),
1925

Bonnard's Nudes

His wife. Forty years he painted her.
Again and again. The nude in the last painting
the same young nude as the first. His wife.

As he remembered her young. As she was young.
His wife in her bath. At her dressing table
in front of the mirror. Undressed.

His wife with her hands under her breasts
looking out on the garden.
The sun bestowing warmth and color.

Every living thing in bloom there.
She young and tremulous and most desirable.
When she died, he painted a while longer.

A few landscapes. Then died.
And was put down next to her.
His young wife.

Raymond Carver, American, 1938–1988

Pierre Bonnard, *Table Set in a Garden* (detail), c. 1908

Sonnet

Here are the bread—the wine—the table—the house:
a man's needs, and a woman's, and a life's.
Peace whirled through and settled in this place:
the common fire burned, to make this light.

Hail to your two hands, which fly and make
their white creations, the singing and the food:
salve! the wholesomeness of your busy feet;
viva! the ballerina who dances with the broom.

Those rugged rivers of water and of threat,
torturous pavilions of the foam,
incendiary hives and reefs: today

they are this respite, your blood in mine,
this path, starry and blue as the night,
this never-ending simple tenderness.

Pablo Neruda, Chilean, 1904–1973
Translated by Alistair Reid

Under the Tree, Here

Under the tree, here,
between green shadows rippling like a stream
and the flagrant eyes of the sun,
the summer morning passes, the summer
passes with its happiness.
Happiness of the wide air, of the clouds
dripping light,
of the gold fruit hanging on the golden boughs.
Happiness of the old heart,
alive, in love.

Diego Valeri, Italian, 1887–1976
Translated by Michael Palma

Martin Johnson Heade, *Cattleya Orchid and Three Brazilian Hummingbirds*, 1871

A Garden beyond Paradise

Everything you see has its roots
    in the Unseen world.
The forms may change,
    yet the essence remains the same.

Every wondrous sight will vanish,
Every sweet word will fade.
    But do not be disheartened,
The Source they come from is eternal—
Growing, branching out,
    giving new life and new joy.

Why do you weep?—
That Source is within you,
And this whole world
    is springing up from it.

The Source is full,
Its waters are ever-flowing;
    Do not grieve,
    drink your fill!
Don't think it will ever run dry—
This is the endless Ocean!

From the moment you came into this world
A ladder was placed in front of you
    that you might escape.

From earth you became plant,
From plant you became animal.
Afterwards you became a human being,
Endowed with knowledge, intellect, and faith.

Behold the body, born of dust—
    how perfect it has become!

Why should you fear its end?
When were you ever made less by dying?

When you pass beyond this human form,
No doubt you will become an angel
And soar through the heavens!

But don't stop there.
Even heavenly bodies grow old.

Pass again from the heavenly realm
and plunge into the vast ocean of
Consciousness.
Let the drop of water that is you
become a hundred mighty seas.

But do not think that the drop alone
Becomes the Ocean—
the Ocean, too, becomes the drop!

Jalal-ud-din Rumi, Persian, 1207–1273
Translated by Jonathan Star and Shahram Shiva

Buddha's Path

This is the Way he traveled to flee the world;
This is the Way he traveled to return to the world.
I, too, come and go along this Sacred Path
That bridges life and death
And traverses illusion.

Ryokan, Japanese, 1758–1831
Translated by John Stevens

Qing Dynasty, *Dish*, 1723–1735

Jacopo Tintoretto, *Christ at the Sea of Galilee*, c. 1575/1580

The Voyage of My Life

The voyage of my life will soon reach,
after stormy seas in a fragile boat,
the common port which all must enter
to give an account of every action, base and noble.
Only now do I see how mistaken
was the beloved illusion
which made art my idol and king
like all things men want to their detriment.

What will become of my amorous longings,
so frivolous and foolish, now that two deaths approach me,
the one certain; the other, a possibility.
Neither painting nor sculpture can soothe
my soul, now turned toward that divine love
who opened his arms on the cross to take us in.

Michelangelo Buonarroti, Italian, 1475–1564

Sassetta and Workshop, *The Meeting of Saint Anthony and Saint Paul*, c. 1440

Hymn to Love

If I speak in the tongues of men and of angels,
    but have not love, I am a noisy gong or
    a clanging cymbal.
And if I have prophetic powers, and understand
    all mysteries and all knowledge, and if I
    have all faith, so as to remove mountains,
    but have not love, I am nothing.
If I give away all I have, and if I deliver my body
    to be burned, but have not love, I gain nothing.
Love is patient and kind; love is not jealous
    or boastful;
It is not arrogant or rude. Love does not insist
    on its own way; it is not irritable or resentful;
It does not rejoice at wrong, but rejoices
    in the right.
Love bears all things, believes all things, hopes
    all things, endures all things.
Love never ends; as for prophecy, it will pass
    away; as for tongues, they will cease; as for
    knowledge, it will pass away.
For our knowledge is imperfect and our
    prophecy is imperfect;
But when the perfect comes, the imperfect will
    pass away.
When I was a child, I spoke like a child, I thought
    like a child, I reasoned like a child; when I
    became a man, I gave up childish ways.
For now we see in a mirror, dimly, but then face to
    face. Now I know in part; then I shall understand
    fully, even as I have been fully understood.
So faith, hope, love abide, these three; but the
    greatest of these is love.

First Letter of Paul to the Corinthians 13:1–13, Revised Standard Version

Oft in the Stilly Night

Oft in the stilly night
    Ere Slumber's chain has bound me,
Fond Memory brings the light
    Of other days around me;
        The smiles, the tears,
        Of boyhood's years,
    The words of love then spoken;
        The eyes that shone,
        Now dimmed and gone,
    The cheerful hearts now broken!
Thus, in the stilly night,
    Ere Slumber's chain has bound me,
Sad Memory brings the light
    Of other days around me.

When I remember all
    The friends so linked together,
I've seen around me fall,
    Like leaves in wintry weather:
        I feel like one
        Who treads alone
    Some banquet-hall deserted,
        Whose lights are fled,
        Whose garland's dead,
And all but he departed!

    Thus in the stilly night,
        Ere Slumber's chain has bound me,
    Fond Memory brings the light
        Of other days around me.

Thomas Moore, English, 1779–1852

Eugène Boudin, *The Beach at Villerville*, 1864

You Came as a Thought

when I was past such thinking
you came as a song when I had

finished singing you came when
the sun had just begun its setting

you were my evening star.

James Laughlin, American, b. 1914

Poem

How could I have come so far
(And always on such dark trails!)
I must have traveled by the light
Shining from the faces of all those I have loved.

Thomas McGrath, American, 1916–1990

He Wanted to Live His Life Over

What? You want to live your life over again?
"Well, I suppose, yes…That time in Grand Rapids…
My life—as I lived it—was a series of shynesses."

Being bolder—what good would that do?
"I'd open my door again. I've felt abashed,
You see. Now I'd go out and say, 'All right,

I'll go with you to Alaska.' Just opening the door
From inside would have altered me—a little.
I'm too shy…" *And so, a bolder life*

Is what you want? "We could begin now.
Just walk with me—down to the river.
I'll pretend this boat is my life…I'll climb in."

Robert Bly, American, b. 1926

The Absolute Solitude

Now at last I've come to touch
the remote edge of eternity

On that edge I rub my eyes
to awake from my long sleep

From my fingertips,
the everlasting stars scatter, their light
gone from my fingertips,
I feel anew the body heat
that comes ever closer to me

Through this heat
I alone embrace the eternity
that ends in me

And from my fingertips
I set adrift like so much dust
the wings of my words lined with soft dreams

I stroke time and gain
with my wrinkled hands
the beautiful eternity that ends in me

And at my fingertips that can reach no further
I keep silent in the end, with my own poems.

Hyonsung Kim, Korean, 1913–1976

Henri Matisse, *Icarus*, published 1947

Ars Poetica

To gaze at the river made of time and water
And recall that time itself is another river,
To know we cease to be, just like the river,
And that our faces pass away, just like the water.

To feel that waking is another sleep
That dreams it does not sleep and that death,
Which our flesh dreads, is that very death
Of every night, which we call sleep.

To see in the day or in the year a symbol
Of mankind's days and of his years,
To transform the outrage of the years
Into a music, a rumor and a symbol,

To see in death a sleep, and in the sunset
A sad gold, of such is Poetry
Immortal and a pauper. For Poetry
Returns like the dawn and the sunset.

At times in the afternoons a face
Looks at us from the depths of a mirror;
Art must be like that mirror
That reveals to us this face of ours.

They tell how Ulysses, glutted with wonders,
Wept with love to descry his Ithaca
Humble and green. Art is that Ithaca
Of green eternity, not of wonders.

It is also like an endless river
That passes and remains, a mirror for one same
Inconstant Heraclitus, who is the same
And another, like an endless river.

Jorge Luis Borges, Argentine, 1899–1986
Translated by Harold Morland

The Last Invocation

At the last, tenderly,
From the walls of the powerful fortress'd house,
From the clasp of the knitted locks, from the keep
    of the well-closed doors,
Let me be wafted.

Let me glide noiselessly forth;
With the key of softness unlock the locks—
    with a whisper,
Set ope the doors O soul.

Tenderly—be not impatient,
(Strong is your hold O mortal flesh.
Strong is your hold O love.)

Walt Whitman, American, 1819–1892

Claude Monet, *The Houses of Parliament, Sunset,* 1903

Acknowledgments

Every effort was made to contact the holders of rights to the poems in this book and to give appropriate credit. Any additions or corrections will be made in future editions if the publisher is notified in writing.

BOA: "I Ask My Mother to Sing," copyright © 1986 by Li-Young Lee. Reprinted from *Rose* with permission of BOA Editions, Ltd., 260 East Avenue, Rochester, New York 14604. "The Lesson of the Falling Leaves," copyright © 1987 by Lucille Clifton. Reprinted from *Good Woman: Poems and a Memoir, 1969-1980* with permission of BOA Editions, Ltd. 260 East Avenue, Rochester New York 14604.

Broken Moon Press: "Your Life," from *The Dance of the Dust on the Rafters: Selections from Ryonyin-hisho.* Translated by Yasuhiko Moriguchi and David Jenkins (Broken Moon Press, 1990). By permission of David Jenkins.

City Lights Books: "Absence" from *Poems of Arab Andalusia.* English translation © copyright 1989 by Cola Franzen. Reprinted by permission of City Lights Books.

Collier Books: "Brown Penny" and "He Wishes for the Cloths of Heaven" reprinted with the permission of Scribner, a Division of Simon & Schuster from *The Collected Works of W. B. Yeats, Volume I: The Poems,* revised and edited by Richard J. Finneran. Copyright © 1983, 1989 by Anne Yeats.

Copper Canyon Press: "Poem" by Thomas McGrath from *Selected Poems, 1938-1988,* © 1988 by Thomas McGrath, reprinted by permission of: Copper Canyon Press, Post Office Box 271, Port Townsend, Washington 98368. "Beach Sandals," "Priceless Gifts," and "To That Which Is Most Important" by Anna Swir from *Talking to My Body,* © 1996, translated by Czeslaw Milosz and Leonard Nathan, reprinted by permission of Copper Canyon Press, Post Office Box 271, Port Townsend, Washington 98368.

Doubleday: "A Man and a Woman Sit Near Each Other" from *Loving a Woman in Two Worlds* by Robert Bly. Copyright © 1985 by Robert Bly. Used by permission of Doubleday, a division of Bantam Doubleday Dell Publishing Group, Inc. "In a Dark Time" copyright © 1960 by Beatrice Roethke, Administratrix of the Estate of Theodore Roethke. From *The Collected Poems of Theodore Roethke* by Theodore Roethke. Used by permission of Doubleday, a division of Bantam Doubleday Dell Publishing Group, Inc.

Farrar, Straus & Giroux, Inc: "Song (4)" from *The Wheel* by Wendell Berry. Copyright © 1982 by Wendell Berry. Reprinted by permission of North Point Press, a division of Farrar, Straus & Giroux, Inc.

Graywolf Press: "Otherwise" copyright 1996 by Jane Kenyon. Reprinted from *Otherwise: New and Selected Poems* with the permission of Graywolf Press, Saint Paul, Minnesota.

Grove Press: "Acrobat about to Enter" from *Love Had a Compass* by Robert Lax. Copyright © 1996 by Robert Lax. Used by permission of Grove/Atlantic, Inc.

Harcourt Brace & Company: "At a Window" from *Chicago Poems* by Carl Sandburg, copyright © 1916 by Holt, Rinehart and Winston and renewed 1944 by Carl Sandburg, reprinted by permission of Harcourt Brace & Company.

HarperCollins Publishers: "I Fell" from *Women in Praise of the Sacred* by Jane Hirshfield, editor. Copyright © 1994 by Jane Hirshfield. Reprinted by permission of HarperCollins Publishers, Inc. "He Wanted to Live His Life Over" from *Morning Poems* by Robert Bly. Copyright © 1997 by Robert Bly. Reprinted by permission of HarperCollins Publishers, Inc.

Henry Holt and Company, Inc: "The Road Not Taken" from *The Poetry of Robert Frost,* edited by Edward Connery Lathem, copyright © 1944 by Robert Frost, copyright 1916, 1969 by Henry Holt and Company, Inc.

Houghton Mifflin Company: "Why the Face of a Clock Is Not Truly a Circle," from *Collected Poems, 1917-1982* by Archibald MacLeish. Copyright © 1985 by the Estate of Archibald MacLeish. Reprinted by permission of Houghton Mifflin Company. All rights reserved.

International Creative Management, Inc: "Bonnard's Nudes" from *Ultramarine.* Reprinted by permission of International Creative Management, Inc. Copyright © 1986 by Raymond Carver; © renewed 1988, 1997.

King's College London: "Mother and Me" by Anna Kamieńska, translated by Krzysztof Piechowicz and Daniel Weissbort from Modern Poetry in Translation, no. 3, 1993.

List of Works of Art

All works of art reproduced in this book are in the collections of the National Gallery of Art, Washington, except as noted.

Ludolf Bakhuysen, *Ships in Distress off a Rocky Coast,* 1667, oil on canvas, Ailsa Mellon Bruce Fund 1985.29.1

William Blake, *The Great Red Dragon and the Woman Clothed with the Sun,* c. 1805, pen and ink with watercolor over graphite, Rosenwald Collection 1943.3.8999

William Blake, from *Songs of Innocence,* 1789, facsimile edition, Trianon Press, 1954, Gift of Lessing J. Rosenwald

Pierre Bonnard, *The Bath,* 1925, lithograph, Rosenwald Collection 1947.12.8

Pierre Bonnard, *The Letter,* c. 1906, oil on canvas, Chester Dale Collection 1963.10.86

Pierre Bonnard, *Table Set in a Garden,* c. 1908, oil on paper mounted on canvas, Ailsa Mellon Bruce Collection 1970.17.8

Botticelli, *Portrait of a Youth,* early 1480s, tempera on panel, Andrew W. Mellon Collection 1937.1.19

Eugène Boudin, *The Beach at Villerville,* 1864, oil on canvas, Chester Dale Collection 1963.10.4

Mary Cassatt, *The Boating Party,* 1893/1894, oil on canvas, Chester Dale Collection 1963.10.94

Mary Cassatt, *Mother and Child,* c. 1905, oil on canvas, Chester Dale Collection 1963.10.98

Paul Cézanne, *Bend in the Road,* 1900-1906, oil on canvas, Collection of Mr. and Mrs. Paul Mellon 1985.64.8

Paul Cézanne, *Still Life,* c. 1900, oil on canvas, Gift of the W. Averell Harriman Foundation in memory of Marie N. Harriman 1972.9.5

Lucille Chabot, *Gabriel Weather Vane,* c. 1939, watercolor on paper, Index of American Design 1943.8.9505

Marc Chagall, *Féla and Odilon,* 1915, gouache and watercolor over black chalk on wove paper, Gift of Evelyn Stefansson Nef in memory of John U. Nef and in Honor of the 50th Anniversary of the National Gallery of Art 1989.85.1
© 1999 Artists Rights Society (ARS), New York/ADAGP, Paris

Jean Siméon Chardin, *Soap Bubbles,* probably 1733/1734, oil on canvas, Gift of Mrs. John W. Simpson 1942.5.1

Thomas Cole, *Sunrise in the Catskills,* 1826, oil on canvas, Gift of Mrs. John D. Rockefeller 3rd, in Honor of the 50th Anniversary of the National Gallery of Art 1989.24.1

Thomas Cole, *The Voyage of Life: Childhood, Youth, Manhood, Old Age,* 1842, Ailsa Mellon Bruce Fund 1971.16.1-4

Jean-Baptiste-Camille Corot, *Ville d'Avray,* c. 1867/1870, oil on canvas, Gift of Count Cecil Pecci-Blunt 1955.9.1

Jasper Francis Cropsey, *Autumn— On the Hudson River,* 1860, oil on canvas, Gift of the Avalon Foundation 1963.9.1

Honoré Daumier, *Advice to a Young Artist,* probably after 1860, oil on canvas, Gift of Duncan Phillips 1941.6.1

Peter Henry Emerson and T. F. Goodall, *Rowing Home the Schoof–Stuff,* 1886, platinum print, from *Life and Landscape on the Norfolk Broads,* 1887, Gift (Partial and Promised) in Honor of the 50th Anniversary of the National Gallery of Art 1995.63.1.U

Walker Evans, *Mount Pleasant, Pennsylvania,* 1935, gelatin silver print, Gift of Mr. and Mrs. Harry Lunn, Jr., in Honor of the 50th Anniversary of the National Gallery of Art 1990.110.8

Walker Evans, *Subway Portrait,* 1938–1941, gelatin silver print, Gift of Kent and Marcia Minichiello, in Honor of the 50th Anniversary of the National Gallery of Art 1990.114.13

Florentine, *Allegorical Portrait of Dante,* late 16th century, oil on panel, Samuel H. Kress Collection 1961.9.57

Jean-Honoré Fragonard, *The Swing*, probably c. 1765, oil on canvas, Samuel H. Kress Collection 1961.9.17

Paul Gauguin, *Breton Girls Dancing, Pont-Aven*, 1888, oil on canvas, Collection of Mr. and Mrs. Paul Mellon 1983.1.19

Vincent van Gogh, *Farmhouse in Provence*, 1888, oil on canvas, Ailsa Mellon Bruce Collection 1970.17.34

Marsden Hartley, *Mount Katahdin, Maine*, 1942, oil on hardboard, Gift of Mrs. Mellon Byers 1970.27.1

Martin Johnson Heade, *Cattleya Orchid and Three Brazilian Hummingbirds*, 1871, oil on wood, Gift of The Morris and Gwendolyn Cafritz Foundation 1982.73.1

Hiroshige, *Bird on a Tree*, color woodcut, Rosenwald Collection 1964.8.1808

Winslow Homer, *Breezing Up (A Fair Wind)*, 1873-1876, oil on canvas, Gift of the W. L. and May T. Mellon Foundation 1943.13.1

Pieter de Hooch, *The Bedroom*, c. 1658/1660, oil on canvas, Widener Collection 1942.9.33

Edward Hopper, *Cape Cod Evening*, 1939, oil on canvas, John Hay Whitney Collection 1982.76.6

Italian, *Playing Cards*, 15th century, woodcut, Rosenwald Collection 1951.16.7

Paul Klee, *New House in the Suburbs*, 1924, gouache on canvas, Collection of Mr. and Mrs. Paul Mellon 1983.1.22

Paul Klee, *Persische Nachtigallen (Persian Nightingales)*, 1917, gouache, watercolor, and pen and ink over graphite on laid paper, Gift (Partial and Promised) in Honor of the 50th Anniversary of the National Gallery of Art 1990.59.2

Gustav Klimt, *Baby (Cradle)*, 1917/1918, oil on canvas, Gift of Otto and Franciska Kallir with help of the Carol and Edwin Gaines Fullinwinder Fund 1978.41.1

Fitz Hugh Lane, *Becalmed off Halfway Rock*, 1860, oil on canvas, Collection of Mr. and Mrs. Paul Mellon, in Honor of the 50th Anniversary of the National Gallery of Art 1992.51.8

Georges de La Tour, *The Repentant Magdalene*, c. 1640, oil on canvas, Ailsa Mellon Bruce Fund 1974.52.1

René Magritte, *La condition humaine*, 1933, oil on canvas, Gift of the Collectors Committee 1987.55.1

Edouard Manet, *Flowers in a Crystal Vase*, c. 1882, oil on canvas, Ailsa Mellon Bruce Collection 1970.17.37

Edouard Manet, *The Railway*, 1873, oil on canvas, Gift of Horace Havemeyer in memory of his mother, Louisine W. Havemeyer 1956.10.1

Edouard Manet, *Still Life with Melon and Peaches*, c. 1866, oil on canvas, Gift of Eugene and Agnes E. Meyer 1960.1.1

Edouard Manet, *The Tragic Actor (Rouvière as Hamlet)*, 1866, oil on canvas Gift of Edith Stuyvesant Gerry 1959.3.1

John Marin, *Untitled: Circus*, c. 1953, oil on canvas, Gift of John Marin, Jr. 1986.54.12

Henri Matisse, *La Coiffure*, 1901, oil on canvas, Chester Dale Collection 1963.10.165 © 1999 Succession H. Matisse, Paris/Artists Rights Society (ARS), New York

Henri Matisse, *Icarus*, published 1947, color stencil in gouache, Gift of Mr. and Mrs. Andrew S. Keck 1980.8.8 © 1999 Succession H. Matisse, Paris/Artists Rights Society (ARS), New York

Henri Matisse, *Pot of Geraniums*, 1912, oil on linen, Chester Dale Collection 1963.10.41 © 1999 Succession H. Matisse, Paris/Artists Rights Society (ARS), New York

Amedeo Modigliani, *Gypsy Woman with Baby*, 1919, oil on canvas, Chester Dale Collection 1963.10.174

Claude Monet, *The Artist's Garden at Vétheuil*, 1880, oil on canvas, Ailsa Mellon Bruce Collection 1970.17.45

Claude Monet, *The Artist's Garden in Argenteuil*, 1873, oil on canvas, Gift (Partial and Promised) in Honor of the 50th Anniversary of the National Gallery of Art 1991.27.1

Claude Monet, *The Cradle—Camille with the Artist's Son Jean*, 1867, oil on canvas, Collection of Mr. and Mrs. Paul Mellon 1983.1.25

Claude Monet, *The Houses of Parliament, Sunset*, 1903, oil on canvas, Chester Dale Collection 1963.10.48

Claude Monet, *Woman with a Parasol— Madame Monet and Her Son*, 1875, oil on canvas, Collection of Mr. and Mrs. Paul Mellon 1983.1.29

Berthe Morisot, *The Artist's Sister at a Window*, 1869, oil on canvas, Ailsa Mellon Bruce Collection 1970.17.47

Berthe Morisot, *The Artist's Sister, Edma, with Her Daughter, Jeanne*, 1872, watercolor over graphite on laid paper, Ailsa Mellon Bruce Collection 1970.17.160

Berthe Morisot, *The Mother and Sister of the Artist*, 1869/1870, oil on canvas, Chester Dale Collection 1963.10.186

Malcolm Morley, *Rite of Passage*, published 1988, spitbite etching, aquatint, and drypoint on John Koller HMP cream paper, Gift of Gemini G.E.L. and the Artist, in Honor of the 50th Anniversary of the National Gallery of Art 1990.71.10

Edvard Munch, *Two Women on the Shore (Frauen am Meeresufer)*, c. 1898, color woodcut with water color, Print Purchase Fund (Rosenwald Collection) and Ailsa Mellon Bruce Fund 1978.15.1

Bartolomé Esteban Murillo, *Two Women at a Window*, c. 1655/1660, oil on canvas, Widener Collection 1942.9.46

Emil Nolde, *Sunflowers, Pink and White Dahlias, and a Blue Delphinium*, c. 1930/1940, watercolor (applied recto and verso) on japan paper, Gift of Margaret Mellon Hitchcock, in Honor of the 50th Anniversary of the National Gallery of Art 1990.73.1

Horace Pippin, *Interior*, 1944, oil on canvas, Gift of Mr. and Mrs. Meyer P. Potamkin, in Honor of the 50th Anniversary of the National Gallery of Art 1991.42.1

Camille Pissarro, *The Artist's Garden at Eragny*, 1898, oil on canvas, Ailsa Mellon Bruce Collection 1970.17.54

Camille Pissarro, *Landscape at Les Pâtis, Pontoise*, 1868, oil on canvas, Gift (Partial and Promised) in Honor of the 50th Anniversary of the National Gallery of Art 1991.101.1

Qing Dynasty, *Dish*, 1723-1735, porcelain with underglaze blue and overglaze doucai enamel decoration, Harry G. Steel Collection, Gift of Grace C. Steele 1972.43.43

Qing Dynasty, *Rectangular Vase Illustrating Poems by Tao Qian and Su Shi*, 1662-1722, porcelain with *famille jaune* and *famille noire* enamels on the biscuit, Widener Collection 1942.9.608

Qing Dynasty, *Shou Lao, the God of Longevity*, 1662-1722, porcelain with *famille verte* enamels on the biscuit, Widener Collection 1942.9.592

Raphael, *Bindo Altoviti*, c. 1515, oil on panel, Samuel H. Kress Collection 1943.4.33

Rembrandt van Rijn, *The Mill*, 1645/1648, oil on canvas, Widener Collection 1942.9.62

Auguste Renoir, *A Girl with a Watering Can*, 1876, oil on canvas, Chester Dale Collection 1963.10.206

Auguste Renoir, *Madame Monet and Her Son*, 1874, oil on canvas, Ailsa Mellon Bruce Collection 1970.17.60

Auguste Renoir, *Picking Flowers*, 1875, oil on canvas, Ailsa Mellon Bruce Collection 1970.17.61

James Rosenquist, *Welcome to the Water Planet*, 1987, aquatint on wove paper, Gift of Graphicstudio/University of South Florida and the Artist, in Honor of the 50th Anniversary of the National Gallery of Art 1990.72.8

Albert Pinkham Ryder, *Siegfried and the Rhine Maidens*, 1888/1891, oil on canvas, Andrew W. Mellon Collection 1946.1.

Sassetta and Workshop, *The Meeting of Saint Anthony and Saint Paul*, c. 1440, tempera on panel, Samuel H. Kress Collection 1939.1.293

Egon Schiele, *Dancer (Die Tänzerin)*, 1913, graphite, watercolor, and gouache on wove paper, Gift (Partial and Promised) in Honor of the 50th Anniversary of the National Gallery of Art 1990.112.1

Georges Seurat, *Seascape at Port-en-Bessin, Normandy*, 1888, oil on canvas, Gift of the W. Averell Harriman Foundation in memory of Marie N. Harriman 1972.9.21

Alfred Sisley, *The Road in the Woods*, 1879, oil on canvas, Chester Dale Collection 1963.10.215

Henry Ossawa Tanner, *The Seine*, c. 1902, oil on canvas, Gift of the Avalon Foundation 1971.57.1

Tintoretto, Jacopo, *Christ at the Sea of Galilee*, c. 1575/1580, oil on canvas, Samuel H. Kress Collection 1952.5.27

Titian, *Venus with a Mirror*, c. 1555, oil on canvas, Andrew W. Mellon Collection 1937.1.34

Joseph Mallord William Turner, *The Dogana and Santa Maria della Salute, Venice*, 1843, oil on canvas, Given in Memory of Governor Alvan T. Fuller by The Fuller Foundation, Inc. 1961.2.3

Joseph Mallord William Turner, *Keelmen Heaving in Coals by Moonlight*, 1835, oil on canvas, Widener Collection 1942.9.86

Johannes Vermeer, *A Lady Writing*, c. 1665, oil on canvas, Gift of Henry Waldron Havemeyer and Horace Havemeyer, Jr., in memory of their father, Horace Havemeyer 1962.10.1

Edouard Vuillard, *Repast in a Garden*, 1898, gouache on cardboard, Chester Dale Collection 1963.10.229

Julian Alden Weir, *Moonlight*, c. 1905, oil on canvas, Chester Dale Collection 1954.4.1

Index of Artists, Authors, and Poems